# THE THREAT OF OVERPOPULATION

BY VALERIE BODDEN

CREATIVE ❦ EDUCATION

Published by Creative Education
P.O. Box 227, Mankato, Minnesota 56002
Creative Education is an imprint of
The Creative Company
www.thecreativecompany.us

Design and production by The Design Lab
Art direction by Rita Marshall
Printed by Corporate Graphics in the
United States of America

Photographs by Alamy (Janos Csernoch,
INTERFOTO, Frans Lemmens), Corbis
(Bernard Bisson/Sygma, Ed Darack/Science
Faction, Historical Picture Archive, Charles &
Josette Lenars, Patrick Robert/Sygma, Kevin
Schafer), Dreamstime (Muratbirsen), Getty
Images (Natalie Behring-Chisholm), iStock-
photo (Steven Allan, Nicholas Belton, Brendan
Bonsack, Imre Cikajlo, Gilles Delmotte, Grant
Dougall, Earl Eliason, Fred Hall, Mark Huls,
Oliver Malms, Chris Pritchard, Uzi Tzur,
Duncan Walker, William Walsh)

Library of Congress
Cataloging-in-Publication Data
Bodden, Valerie.
The threat of overpopulation / by Valerie
Bodden.
p. cm. — (Earth issues)
Includes bibliographical references and index.
Summary: An examination of the environmen-
tal threats an unsustainable human popula-
tion presents, exploring the effects of pollution
and overcrowding, as well as how people can
contribute to a healthier planet.
ISBN 978-1-58341-983-0
1. Overpopulation—Juvenile literature. 2.
Overpopulation—Environmental aspects—Ju-
venile literature. I. Title. II. Series.

HB883.B63 2010
363.9'1—dc22          2009028052

CPSIA: 120109 PO1091
First Edition
9 8 7 6 5 4 3 2 1

# Table of Contents

Everything human beings need to survive—air to breathe, food to eat, water to drink—is found on Earth, and on Earth alone. Yet the very planet that sustains human life has come under threat because of human activities. Rivers are drying up as people divert water for their own use. Temperatures are warming as greenhouse gases such as carbon dioxide trap heat in the **atmosphere**. Species of plants and animals are disappearing as people destroy essential habitats. And the rate of many such changes appears to be accelerating. "If I had to use one word to describe the environmental state of the planet right now, I think I would say precarious," said population expert Robert Engelman. "It isn't doomed. It isn't certainly headed toward disaster. But it's in a very precarious situation right now."

With the globe's population at nearly 6.8 billion people, many scientists fear that the sheer number of human beings on Earth may be one of the planet's biggest threats. They see overpopulation as the cause of nearly all environmental problems—from pollution to global warming to the loss of **biodiversity**—that plague Earth. And as the planet's population continues to grow, some fear that the human population will eventually reach a level that Earth simply cannot sustain—indeed, some scientists believe we have already reached that level. But how fast is Earth's population growing? And how does population growth affect the natural world and the humans who inhabit it? Is there any way to keep overpopulation from overextending Earth's resources?

The world's population has not always been as large as it is today. For several centuries before the birth of Christ, the global population grew slowly, reaching a total of 250 million sometime around the first century A.D. It took another 1,600 years for the population to double to 500 million. Then, in the mid-17th century, population growth gradually began to pick up speed, largely because improvements in nutrition, hygiene, and medicine helped to increase life expectancy. By 1850 or so, the global population had reached one billion, and almost 100 years later, around 1930, another billion people had been added to the planet. After World War II ended in 1945, the development of infection-fighting antibiotics, vaccines for diseases such as smallpox and measles, and improvements in water safety and sanitation led to a dramatic drop in death rates around the world. As a result, the global population reached three billion by 1960. Since then, the time period needed to add another billion people to the world's population has grown even shorter; the four-billion mark was reached in 1974, five billion in 1986, and six billion in 1999.

CHAPTER ONE

# Growing by Leaps and Bounds

When **demographers** look at world population growth, however, they do not look only at how long it takes for the population to reach certain milestones. They also analyze the global rate of growth. Until the mid-1700s, the world's population probably grew at a rate of 0.5 percent or less each year. By 1930, the growth rate probably reached about 1 percent per year, and it peaked around 2.1 percent in the mid-1960s. Today, the world grows at a rate of about 1.2 percent each year. This does not mean that the number of people in the world has decreased, however. The world's population is so large that a growth rate of

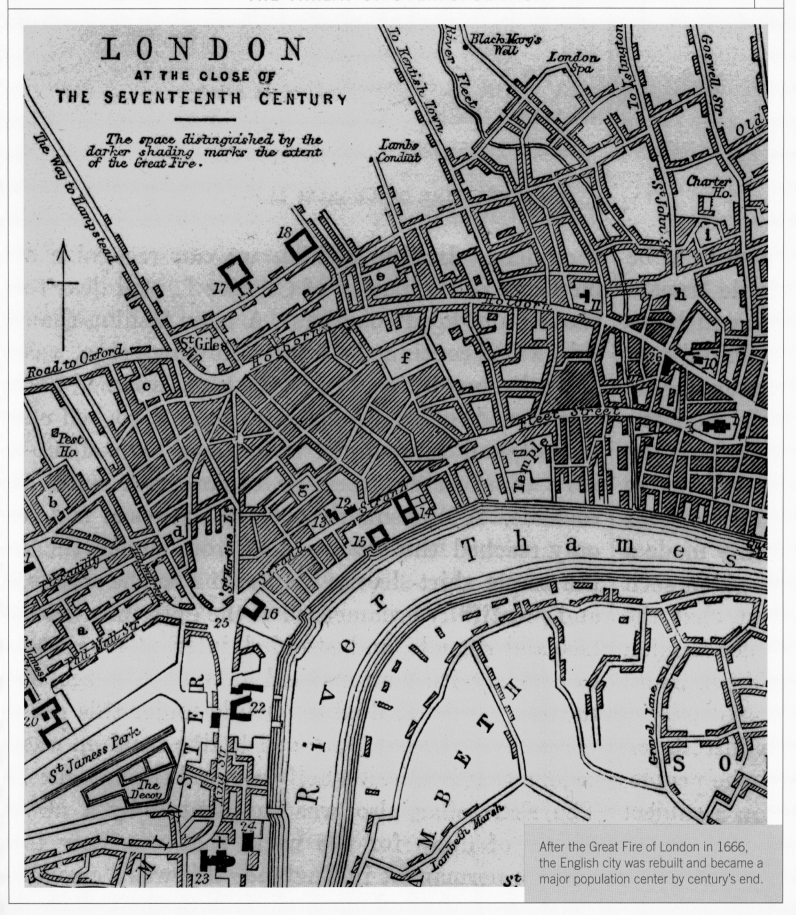

LONDON
AT THE CLOSE OF
THE SEVENTEENTH CENTURY

The space distinguished by the darker shading marks the extent of the Great Fire.

After the Great Fire of London in 1666, the English city was rebuilt and became a major population center by century's end.

The area of Johannesburg, South Africa, known as Soweto is so crowded that settlements of shacks spring up amidst the houses.

1.2 percent means that approximately 81 million people are added to the population every year, or more than 220,000 each day.

The reason that Earth's population continues to grow can be explained by the total fertility rate, or the average number of children born to each woman over her lifetime. The higher the fertility rate, the faster a population will grow (assuming there isn't a corresponding dramatic increase in the **mortality rate**). Fertility rates below two can eventually lead to population decline. A fertility rate of 2.1 is considered the replacement rate—the number of children needed to replace both parents and hold population levels steady (the number is more than two to account for infant mortality). Worldwide, the average fertility rate today is 2.6 children per woman (down from 4.8 in the 1970s), but fertility rates vary drastically around the globe. In all of the world's **developed countries**, fertility is at

As a national symbol, the American flag signifies the freedoms U.S. citizens enjoy—and also the lifestyle many other countries want.

## People Problems

No one has yet been able to determine Earth's carrying capacity, or the total number of people the planet can support. Estimates over the past 100 years have ranged from fewer than 1 billion to more than 1 trillion, with the majority of guesses between 4 and 16 billion. One reason for the uncertainty is that the carrying capacity depends in large part on human consumption—the more each person consumes, the fewer people Earth can support. According to some demographers, if everyone in the world were to experience the standards of living enjoyed by Americans, the planet could support only 1.5 to 2 billion people.

or below the replacement level—in some cases, well below. Japan, Belarus, Poland, and Ukraine exhibit exceptionally low fertility levels of fewer than 1.5 children per woman. In the **developing world**, however, fertility levels tend to be higher. Eleven countries—among them Afghanistan, the Democratic Republic of the Congo, Niger, Somalia, and Uganda—have fertility levels of six or more children per woman.

Just as the fertility rate varies from place to place, so too does the population. Nearly half of the world's people live in just seven countries: China, India, the United States, Indonesia, Brazil, Pakistan, and Nigeria. China is the world's most populous nation, with more than 1.3 billion people, followed closely by India at more than 1.1 billion. The U.S. is a distant third, with approximately 307 million people. The majority of the world's most populous nations (with the notable exception of the U.S.) are in the developing world. In fact, 80 percent of the world's population lives in the developing countries of Africa, Asia, and Latin America, and these regions also account for 95 percent of total population growth.

On another level, countries also vary in population density—a measure of how many people live in a specific area. A small country with a large population has a greater density than a large country with a small population. The small island nation of Singapore, for example, has a density of 17,650 people per square mile (6,814 per sq km). Libya, on the other hand, has a population of 6.2 million spread across one of the largest countries in Africa. Its population density is only 9.2 people per square mile (3.6 per sq km). People do not settle evenly across a country, however, so population density varies from location to location even within a specific nation. In Libya, for example, most of the population lives near the coast of the Mediterranean Sea, leaving

Despite Singapore's staggeringly high population density, the aging nation has the third-lowest fertility rate in the world, at 1.26.

much of the rest of the country uninhabited. The most densely populated regions of a country are its urban areas, or cities.

In 2008, for the first time in history, half of the world's population was settled in urban areas, meaning that the growth of cities—known as urbanization—has far outpaced overall population growth. One of the reasons for the rapid growth of cities is the natural increase in population through births to urban women. But migration from the countryside to cities is also a factor, as is the transformation of rural areas into cities.

## People Problems

People today are not the first to express concerns about overpopulation. An ancient Babylonian poem warned that overpopulation could lead to catastrophe, while the ancient Greek philosophers Plato and Aristotle cautioned that population growth could lead to scarcity of resources and poverty. In the third century B.C., Chinese philosopher Han Fei-Tzu wrote that as people had more children, there was less wealth to go around. In 1798, British economist Thomas Malthus warned that population growth would eventually exceed Earth's capacity to produce food. Today, people who believe that the world is in the midst of a population crisis are sometimes referred to as Malthusians.

Clergyman and scholar Thomas Malthus's most well-known work was his 1798 book *An Essay on the Principle of Population.*

In the developed world, nearly 75 percent of the population already lives in urban areas, and countries such as the U.S. and Australia are expected to be 90 percent urban by 2050. Although Africa and Asia remain largely rural, their rapidly growing cities are home to more than 60 percent of the world's urban population. Developing countries in Asia and Latin America are also home to the majority of the world's 26 megacities (**metropolitan areas** with a population greater than 10 million), such as Mexico City, Mexico; Mumbai, India; and São Paulo, Brazil. The two largest megacities are in the developed world, however. The **urban agglomeration** of Tokyo, Japan, has a total population of 33.8 million, and Seoul, South Korea, holds 23.9 million residents. Despite their huge populations, megacities account for only about 13 percent of all urban dwellers in the world. More than half of the world's urban population lives in cities of 500,000 or fewer residents.

Approximately 50 years after Babylon was conquered by the Greeks (in 331 B.C.), the city's census showed a population of 600,000.

## People Problems

In order to determine their population, most countries conduct censuses, or regular counts of their people. Some of the world's first censuses were probably taken by the Babylonians and the Chinese during the fourth century B.C. The oldest census record still in existence dates from 1427 in Tuscany, an Italian region, and by the late 18th and early 19th centuries, the U.S. and Britain had begun to regularly count their populations. Other countries began to record censuses during the late 19th or early 20th centuries. Because it is impossible for any census to attain complete accuracy, as people are constantly being born and dying, population figures are always rough estimates.

With so many people now inhabiting the planet, few places remain completely untouched by human activities. Because of this fact, some scientists believe that overpopulation is the direct cause of a number of environmental problems. In 1993, 58 academies of science from around the world issued a joint statement claiming "the magnitude of the threat ... is linked to human population size and resource use per person.... As human numbers further increase, the potential for irreversible changes of far-reaching magnitude also increases."

CHAPTER TWO

# Changing the World

Air pollution is one of the environmental problems blamed at least in part on overpopulation. Although the air in developed cities such as Pittsburgh, Pennsylvania, and Tokyo is now cleaner than it once was, cities in the developing world are today suffering from massive levels of air pollution. Manila, the capital of the Philippines, for example, is one of the world's most polluted cities, with air pollution levels four times higher than the nation's air standards.

In many of the world's least developed countries, one of the principal sources of air pollution is the burning of coal and other plant- or animal-based fuels for cooking or heating homes, which affects both outdoor and indoor air quality. Industry is another significant source of air pollution, especially in developing nations where environmental laws tend to be lax. Among the 20 cities in the world with the worst air pollution, 16 are located in the rapidly industrializing country of China. Worldwide, automobiles account for a high percentage of air pollutants. In São Paulo, vehicles contribute to 90 percent of the thick, dark smog (a mixture of smoke, fog, and other air pollutants) that blankets the city, and in Mexico City, cars are responsible for 75 percent of air

Not only is the health of its residents adversely affected, but a city's architecture and natural beauty can be obscured by smog as well.

pollution. Despite the fact that developed nations have reduced the amount of emissions produced by their vehicle engines, they are not free from automobile pollution problems. Urbanization in developed nations such as the U.S. often leads to sprawl, or the spread of cities and low-density **suburbs** far into surrounding areas. As a result, people must rely on cars to get from one location to another, drastically increasing the number of miles driven (and thus the number of pollutants emitted) each year.

Many scientists believe that overpopulation not only increases air pollution but also adds to the threat of global warming, which is believed to be caused by excessive emissions of greenhouse gases such as carbon dioxide into the atmosphere. They reason that, with more people on Earth, more greenhouse gases will be released as those people burn fossil fuels such as coal or oil for heat, cooking, and transportation. Many people worry that growing cities pose a particular threat to the stability of the global climate, since urban areas already contribute the majority of the world's greenhouse gas emissions. Cities can also cause local climate change through what is known as the heat island effect. Because of their high concentration of buildings and roads, heat emissions from cars and factories, and lack of greenery, cities tend to be hotter than surrounding areas. In New York City, for example, the average nighttime temperature is 7 °F (3.9 °C) warmer than that of nearby rural areas. The heat island effect can also increase the amount of energy used for air conditioning, impact water resources, and contribute to the formation of smog.

From traffic crossing its bridges to electricity lighting its buildings, a lot of energy is consumed in a city such as New York.

In the outskirts of large urban areas such as Dhaka, Bangladesh, pollution is a common sight for—and danger to—the children who grow up there.

Earth's waterways also often suffer from pollution related to overpopulation. In many cases, urban industries discharge their waste directly into rivers or lakes. Individuals also pollute waterways in many areas, especially in overcrowded, undeveloped cities, where public waste disposal and sanitation services are not available. And when people settle near coasts—as half the world's population already has—**silt**, waste, and other pollutants are discharged into the oceans and seas, endangering coral reefs and fish habitats.

Pollution is just one way in which the growing human population endangers natural habitats. As cities expand to accommodate ever-increasing numbers of people, natural habitats are often destroyed to make room: wetlands are drained or filled, forests are cut down, and rivers are dammed. In São Paulo, expanding urban growth on the city's fringes has led to high levels of deforestation. Even when entire habitats aren't destroyed, sprawl often results in habitat fragmentation, or the slicing of a habitat into small, isolated pieces.

While Earth's growing cities play a large part in the loss of natural habitats, rural areas carry much of the blame as well. Producing enough food to provide for all of the planet's people has required large areas of land to be converted into agricultural fields. Today, few of the world's grasslands remain in their natural state, and forests in tropical regions continue to be chopped down to develop land for farming.

Ironically, although agriculture has been pegged as one of the reasons for the loss of natural habitats, agriculture itself is sometimes threatened by the growth of cities. In the U.S., for example, more than one million acres (404,685 ha) of farmland are converted into suburban neighborhoods each year. As a result of such urban sprawl, more food must be grown on less land, or land

## People Problems

As its rapid pace of urbanization continues, China has announced plans to build what it calls the world's first "eco-city," which will be located on an island in the Yangtze River near Shanghai. Windmills, solar energy, and combusted waste will produce much of the city's power, and vehicles in the city will be required to run on electricity or fuel cells. The city, called Dongtan, will also have an extensive system of public transportation and bicycle and walking paths, which should keep its vehicle emissions near zero. Although the building schedule calls for 500,000 people to live in Dongtan by 2050, construction had not yet begun as of 2009.

unsuitable for farming must be brought under cultivation. Either option increases the pressure on the land and forces farmers to use more chemical fertilizers or **irrigation** water, which can cause further damage to local **ecosystems**.

The loss of ecosystems due to expanding human populations has had a significant impact on the plants and animals that inhabit the planet. Habitat destruction, fragmentation, and **degradation** are leading causes of species endangerment and extinction. In California, for example, population growth and urban sprawl have destroyed all but 10 percent of the Mediterranean coastal sage **scrubland** habitat, which supports a high number of **endemic** species. What habitat remains is fragmented, preventing animal populations from moving freely to find food or mates.

Increased food consumption coupled with ever-growing populations around the world drive up demand for more farmland.

Many demographers believe that the sheer number of people on Earth is only one reason overpopulation threatens the planet's resources. Another is that human **consumption** continues to increase. As more people consume more goods, more of Earth's resources are used up. As might be expected, people in the developed world, who are generally wealthier, are the biggest consumers. In fact, according to American entomologist and population studies expert Paul Ehrlich, because the U.S. has a large population and a high rate of consumption, "it is fair to say that the United States is the most overpopulated country on the planet." Consumption levels in developing countries such as China, India, and Mexico are beginning to rise, too, as incomes increase. Many "new consumers" in these countries are buying cars for the first time and are beginning to eat more meat.

Too many people consuming too many resources doesn't affect the natural world alone. It also has consequences for the people who live in it. Poverty, hunger, disease, natural disasters, and political instability have all been blamed at least in part on overpopulation. While poverty is often the result of injustice, corruption, and ineffective government, some experts believe that overpopulation also plays a role. Today, nearly half of the people in the world survive on less than $.50 a day. One of the most pronounced results of poverty is hunger. Each year, nearly one billion people in the world go hungry, and **malnutrition** contributes to the deaths of nearly six million children under the age of five. According to some experts, enough food is currently produced to feed the entire population of the world, but many people either cannot afford to buy enough food to eat or cannot grow enough to provide for their families. In addition, some experts contend that as the human population continues to grow and as progress is made toward improving nutrition worldwide, agricultural production will have to increase dramatically in order to provide everyone with enough food.

CHAPTER THREE

# Overpopulation and People

Seventy-five percent of the world's hungry live in rural areas, but urban populations also suffer from malnutrition and other forms of poverty. Most of the urban poor live in slums or shantytowns on the edges of urban areas. It is estimated that worldwide slum populations are close to one billion. Most slums are informal or illegal settlements where poor residents often patch together homes from whatever materials they can find. In Abidjan, Ivory Coast, for example, slum homes are made of cardboard, with metal roofs. Often, several families crowd into one-room

The West African city of Abidjan experienced economic growth until the 1980s but has a large population living in slum conditions.

Because China has nearly 50 cities with populations greater than 1 million, tall, crowded apartment buildings are often the best use of space.

dwellings that lack even the most basic electric, water, or sanitation services. The crowded, unsanitary state of slums makes them ideal places for the spread of illnesses and conditions such as diarrhea, pneumonia, cholera, and typhus. As a result, 10 percent of urban children in developing countries die before the age of 5.

Pollution is yet another cause of illness and death in overpopulated countries. Among the effects of air pollution are asthma, bronchitis, and other respiratory diseases. Some air pollutants, called **volatile organic compounds**, can also damage the cardiac and reproductive systems; lead to low birth weight, birth defects, and developmental disabilities in babies; or even cause cancer. The World Health Organization (WHO) estimates that air pollution is responsible for about two million deaths a year, largely in rapidly urbanizing nations. In China alone, up to 656,000 people a year are believed to be killed by the effects of air pollution. Developed nations are not free of pollution-related deaths, either. More than 40,000 deaths a year in Austria, France, and Switzerland combined are believed to be due to air pollution, with about half attributable to vehicle emissions.

Apart from its problems with overpopulation, Easter Island is most known for its curious and ancient statues called *moai*.

## People Problems

Demographers who believe that overpopulation could lead to resource scarcity and warfare often point to the case of Easter Island. Located in the South Pacific Ocean, Easter Island is believed to have grown slowly from the time it was settled in the early centuries A.D. until about 1100, when its population began to double every 100 years. By 1600, the population had reached 6,000 to 8,000 people. By then, the island had been completely deforested, and fresh water was in short supply. Fights soon broke out over scarce resources, and the conflicts, combined with disease, wiped out all but 111 of the island's people by 1877.

## People Problems

Founded in 1969, the United Nations Population Fund (UNFPA) aims to "ensure that every pregnancy is wanted, every birth is safe, every young person is free of HIV/AIDS, and every girl and woman is treated with dignity and respect." Working in 150 countries around the world, the UNFPA supports governments in using population data to develop strategies to reduce poverty and increase sustainability. By 2015, the organization hopes to help governments provide all people with access to reproductive health services, ensure that all children receive a primary education, and reduce maternal mortality (the number of women who die during pregnancy or childbirth) by 75 percent.

More than 11 million African children have lost their parents to AIDS and need assistance from groups such as UNFPA.

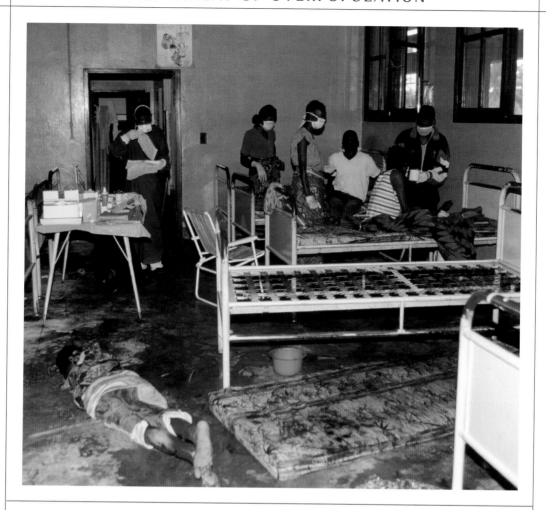

A 1995 outbreak of the Ebola virus overwhelmed medical workers in Kikwit, Democratic Republic of the Congo, killing 245.

People living in cities are not the only ones vulnerable to the health effects of overpopulation. As human populations spread into previously uninhabited areas, people come into closer contact with animals that carry diseases. Many of these animals can be found in the world's tropical rainforests; both AIDS and the **Ebola virus** are thought to have originally been transferred to human beings through contact with rainforest animals. With populations pressed close to one another and people from other regions of the world able to easily travel to Africa and other tropical destinations, such diseases can quickly spread to infect large numbers of people.

While overpopulation can directly threaten human health, it can also indirectly endanger the planet's "ecosystem services" that help to sustain human life. Ecosystems and the plants and animals that live within them provide food, produce oxygen, cycle and purify fresh water, reduce flooding, prevent soil erosion, and regulate Earth's climate. When overpopulation leads to damage of Earth's ecosystems, it also impairs their ability to provide such services. In Jakarta, Indonesia, for example, increasing urbanization has led to the destruction of vegetation along the banks of the Ciliwung River. As a result, the soil along the river has eroded into the waterway, making it narrower and shallower. An increase in roadways and other paved areas means that when it rains, water flows into the river, rather than soaking into the ground. Together, these two factors often result in flooding that affects hundreds of thousands of residents.

Vulnerability to floods and other natural disasters tends to increase as populations grow, especially in cities in the developing world. Part of the reason for this is that many cities do not have the **infrastructure** needed to prepare for and respond to disasters. Poorly built houses and densely packed neighborhoods can also contribute to the threat. The location of cities is also often a factor. Several of the world's most populous cities sit on or near earthquake

The hillside town of Balakot, Pakistan, had a population of 20,000 prior to a 2005 earthquake, which left it in absolute ruins.

faults, while others are situated near volcanoes. Landslides can also be a threat when overpopulation forces poorer residents to settle on steep hillsides. In 1998, Hurricane Mitch killed thousands of people living in mountainside slums in Nicaragua and Honduras. In the future, residents of coastal cities are likely to be at risk from rising sea levels due to global warming. Climate change, combined with the heat island effect, could also lead to an increase in deadly heat waves, such as the one that killed at least 30,000 Europeans in 2003. Fire can also be a threat in cities, and especially in slums, where people cook over open fires in closely packed homes made of flammable materials.

Some people worry that other problems will increase as Earth's population continues to grow. The conflict over increasingly scarce resources such as water, food, and energy has the potential to lead to political instability and civil unrest. It could even develop into full-scale wars as governments fight to provide for their people. Some experts have suggested that the ongoing conflict between ethnic groups in the Darfur region of Sudan is at least in part a result of overpopulation and tensions over limited resources.

The effects of Hurricane Mitch were at first visible in the destroyed homes but also later felt in Honduras's economic distress.

No one knows how large Earth's population will grow, but most demographers agree that the planet's population cannot continue to increase endlessly. Already, population growth is starting to decline in many areas of the world, and developed countries such as Germany, Italy, and Japan are expected to have smaller populations in 2050 than they do today. Many countries in the developing world are also experiencing declining fertility rates. The United Nations (UN) projects that even if fertility rates continue to decline, the world's population will still reach more than nine billion by 2050; if fertility rates remain constant, the number could be much higher. Demographers anticipate that nearly all population growth will occur in urban areas of developing nations.

CHAPTER FOUR

# An End in Sight?

Although fertility rates in many parts of the world have begun to fall, some demographers believe that more needs to be done in order to slow and eventually stop population growth. Some fear that if the number of births in the world isn't limited further, then the number of deaths will greatly increase as Earth's resources are overextended and can no longer support everyone on the planet. The goal that most of these demographers would like to see reached is zero population growth; others would even like to see the population of the planet sink below current levels.

Many countries around the world have instituted policies aimed at reducing fertility rates. Such programs often include providing **contraceptives** to couples. Worldwide, contraceptives are used by 63 percent of women who are married or in a relationship, but this rate varies greatly from country to country, with the lowest levels in sub-Saharan Africa. Population experts have also recently begun to understand that providing increased

Although Japanese families may be small, the people hold on tightly to their traditions, such as wearing kimonos for festivals.

## People Problems

While many countries want to lower their fertility rate, some want to raise it. More than 20 developed countries in Europe, along with Japan, believe their populations are not growing enough. They fear that a smaller population could mean a weaker army or a shrunken economy. Some also worry that, as fewer babies are born, the majority of their population will consist of older citizens, which could lead to labor shortages or an inability to fund **pension** programs. In order to encourage families to have more children, some governments have offered cash bonuses, money for child care, tax credits, or flexible work schedules for parents.

## People Problems

In the mid-1970s, the government of India adopted a harsh population control policy that allowed states to fine or imprison couples who refused to be **sterilized** after having three or more children. Many Indian states also required individuals to present proof that they had been sterilized in order to receive housing, electricity, or medical care. In some villages, men were rounded up and forcibly taken to sterilization camps, no matter how many children they had had or whether they were married or not. Hundreds died from mistakes made during sterilizations, and those who protested the population program were often arrested or killed.

The Indian government posted signs that reminded people what the ideal family should look like as it imposed population control.

educational and job opportunities for females can lower fertility rates. Improving health care to reduce child mortality can also decrease the fertility rate, since in many countries, parents have several children to ensure that some will survive past youth. Some governments have even rewarded couples who choose to have fewer children. The state of Andhra Pradesh in India, for example, gives cash, houses, land, or loans to those who are sterilized after having one or two children.

In other countries, people are not rewarded for having fewer children, but they are punished for having more. China, for example, implemented a one-child policy in the late 1970s, imposing severe fines on those who violated the rule. In some cases, the policy even led to forced abortions and sterilizations. While some population experts have applauded the policy's success in lowering China's fertility rate from nearly 6 children per woman in 1970 to 1.7 today, others have denounced China's policy as a human rights abuse. The country announced in 2007 that it would increase fines for wealthy families who ignored the policy (while poor farming families are sometimes allowed to have two children, especially if the firstborn is a girl, so that they will have more help for farm labor).

In addition to slowing population growth overall, some demographers believe that efforts must be made to slow the growth of cities by reducing the number of people migrating to them. Increasing rural job opportunities, improving farm productivity, and providing rural infrastructure can all help to stem the flow of people into cities. In rural areas around the city of Timbuktu in the African nation of Mali, for example, residents have been encouraged to grow eucalyptus and bourgou (an aquatic grass), which they sell to residents in the city for use as construction material, fuel, and animal food. As a result, rural incomes in the area have increased dramatically, leading most rural dwellers to stay put.

Some researchers, however, have suggested that rather than discouraging urbanization, governments should allow large cities to continue to grow, provided that they improve infrastructure. They point out that cities often provide their citizens with higher incomes, better health care, and more educational opportunities. Of course, before they can offer these advantages, cities must first be able to take care of all citizens' basic needs, such as housing, water, and sanitation. By providing small, affordable plots of land connected to city services, along with loans or materials for housing, cities can make great strides in improving the lives of their poorest citizens.

Outside the famed—but now impoverished—city of Timbuktu, gardeners have to carry water to their plants to combat the desert heat.

When bicycles cannot have entire streets to themselves, a designated bike lane is a good alternative to mixing with motorized city traffic.

## People Problems

High fertility rates are one reason that the world's population has grown so rapidly in recent centuries, but another factor is the fall in death rates. During the first few centuries A.D., average life expectancy was around 22 years but increased to 30 years by 1800. A century later, life expectancy had risen to 40 or 50 years in North America and northwestern Europe. Today, life expectancy in developed countries is around 76 years, while residents of the least developed nations have a life expectancy of 53 years. In recent times, the life expectancy in some African countries has decreased, largely due to the spread of AIDS.

In many developed nations, where residents already enjoy a relatively high standard of living, the focus is placed not on providing basic services but on reducing the effects of urbanization on the environment. Countries such as the U.S. are working to reduce sprawl by restoring and revitalizing downtown areas, developing suburbs with higher population densities, and increasing transit options. Several cities have created electrical rail systems, along with cycleways for bikes. In Denmark and the Netherlands, for example, entire streets are devoted to bicycle traffic. New urban buildings are constructed to conserve energy through the use of solar power and other renewable resources. Green areas covered with trees and other plants are being restored in many cities, including on the rooftops of buildings. In some cities, many of these plants are grown for food in a practice known as urban farming.

Even older homes in cities can practice urban farming—to an extent—if there is space enough for a small backyard garden.

Although urban farming can help to provide new sources of food for the world's growing population, many people believe that feeding a population that could potentially reach more than nine billion will require technological advances in agriculture. Some point to genetically modified (GM) foods as the answer. When scientists genetically modify foods, they take **genes** from other wild or cultivated plants and insert them into a crop plant in order to improve its ability to resist pests, make it fast-growing, or increase its yield. Some scientists worry, however, that GM foods will not increase the world's food supply enough to provide all people with an adequate diet.

In addition to addressing overpopulation, urbanization, and food production, many demographers feel that the world needs to find a way to solve the problem of overconsumption. Today, most people in developed nations continue to seek more and better products, while those in developing countries strive to achieve the consumption patterns modeled by wealthier nations. One solution offered by some economists is to levy high taxes on environmentally harmful products, such as fossil fuels and inefficient appliances, in order to discourage their consumption.

According to many demographers, both consumption and population must be reduced —and soon—in order to save both the planet and its inhabitants. Population studies expert Paul Ehrlich believes that "we can set aside reserves for biodiversity until we're blue in the face, burn fossil fuels ever more efficiently, and recycle assiduously [carefully], and civilization will still go down the environmental drain unless population and consumption are addressed." Fortunately, many people today are working to tackle these issues, meaning that our planet may be a less populated but more sustainable one in the foreseeable future.

Household waste is one of the biggest problems facing an overpopulated world, and many cities do not know how best to dispose of it.

## People Problems

Demographers study not only the number of people in a population but also specific facts about those people, including their age. People between the ages of 15 and 59 make up a country's working population. In most of the world, about 50 to 60 percent of the population is of working age. In the countries of the developing world, where populations are increasing quickly, a large proportion of the population (up to 50 percent in some African nations) is under the age of 15. In contrast, nations with declining fertility rates have an aging population. Today, 20 percent of the developed world's population is 60 or older.

If children in developing countries can survive to become healthy, working adults, they can perhaps change their own children's fate.

# Glossary

**atmosphere**—the layer of gases that surrounds Earth

**biodiversity**—the variety of life in the world or in a certain habitat

**consumption**—the purchase and use of products and services

**contraceptives**—methods or devices intended to keep a woman from becoming pregnant by preventing sperm from fertilizing an egg; condoms are one type of contraceptive

**degradation**—the process of breaking down or declining in quality

**demographers**—people who study statistics such as population size, growth, distribution, density, and makeup

**developed countries**—the wealthier nations of the world, which are generally characterized by high individual incomes, along with high levels of education and industrialization

**developing world**—having to do with the poorest countries of the world, which are generally characterized by a lack of health care, nutrition, education, and industry; most developing countries are in Africa, Asia, and Latin America

**Ebola virus**—an infective agent spread through bodily fluids such as blood that causes a deadly disease marked by bleeding inside the body and fever

**ecosystems**—communities of organisms that depend on one another and interact with their environment

**endemic**—of a plant or animal species that is native to a narrowly defined geographic region such as a specific island or mountain

**genes**—the basic units of heredity that transmit traits or characteristics from parents to offspring

**infrastructure**—a society's basic physical structures and facilities, such as buildings and roads

**irrigation**—the distribution of water to land or crops to help plant growth

**malnutrition**—lack of needed nutrients due to not having enough to eat or not eating enough of the right foods, leading to physical harm to the body

**metropolitan areas**—population centers made up of a city and its surrounding towns and suburbs

**mortality rate**—the number of deaths in a certain area or period of time, or from a certain cause

**pension**—a regular payment made to a person who has retired from his or her job

**scrubland**—an area consisting of scrub vegetation, or low trees and shrubs

**silt**—very fine particles of mud or clay carried by rivers and deposited as sediment

**sterilized**—made infertile (unable to produce children) through a surgical procedure

**suburbs**—residential areas on the outskirts of larger cities

**urban agglomeration**—a continuously built-up area consisting of a cluster or mass of cities built close together

**volatile organic compounds**—chemical compounds present in substances such as paint that contain the element carbon and that evaporate at low temperatures, releasing gases that cause air pollution

# Bibliography

Cohen, Joel. *How Many People Can the Earth Support?* New York: W. W. Norton, 1995.

Connelly, Matthew. *Fatal Misconception: The Struggle to Control World Population.* Cambridge, Mass.: Harvard University Press, 2008.

Ehrlich, Paul, and Anne Ehrlich. *One with Nineveh: Politics, Consumption, and the Human Future.* Washington, D.C.: Island Press, 2004.

Johnson, Elizabeth, and Michael Klemens, eds. *Nature in Fragments: The Legacy of Sprawl.* New York: Columbia University Press, 2005.

Moffett, George. *Critical Masses: The Global Population Challenge.* New York: Viking, 1994.

Soule, David, ed. *Urban Sprawl: A Comprehensive Reference Guide.* Westport, Conn.: Greenwood Press, 2006.

Starke, Linda, ed. *2007 State of the World: Our Urban Future.* New York: W. W. Norton, 2007.

United Nations. "Department of Economic and Social Affairs, Population Division." United Nations. http://www.un.org/esa/population/unpop.htm.

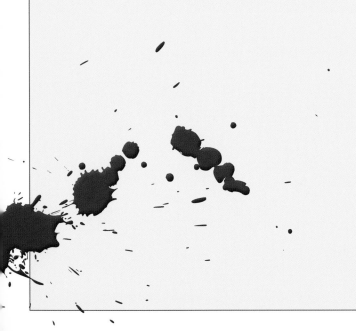

# For Further Information

## Books

Bowden, Rob. *Cities*. San Diego: KidHaven Press, 2004.

———. *An Overcrowded World?: Our Impact on the Planet*.
Austin, Tex.: Raintree Steck-Vaughn Publishers, 2002.

Lomberg, Michelle. *Healthy Cities: Improving Urban Life*. North
Mankato, Minn.: Smart Apple Media, 2004.

Mason, Paul. *Population*. Chicago: Heinemann Library, 2006.

## Web Sites

National Geographic Eye in the Sky: Overpopulation
http://www.nationalgeographic.com/eye/overpopulation/overpopulation.html

United Nations Cyberschoolbus: City Profiles
http://www.un.org/Pubs/CyberSchoolBus/habitat/profiles/index.asp

United Nations Cyberschoolbus: Country at a Glance
http://cyberschoolbus.un.org/infonation/index.asp

The World Almanac for Kids: Population
http://www.worldalmanacforkids.com/WAKI-Chapter.aspx?chapter_id=10

# Index